THE
COLLABORATIVE
ARTIST

Joy to the World

Georg Friedrich Händel

arranged by Nancy Faber

FLUTE

CELLO

PIANO

FABER
PIANO ADVENTURES

ISBN 978-1-61677-706-7

"Joy to the World, the Lord is come!
Let earth receive her King;
Let every heart prepare Him room,
And Heaven and nature sing,
And Heaven and nature sing,
And Heaven, and Heaven, and nature sing."

~Isaac Watts, 1719

Joy to the World
for Flute, Cello, and Piano

Georg Friedrich Händel
arranged by Nancy Faber

Allegro (♩ = 116)

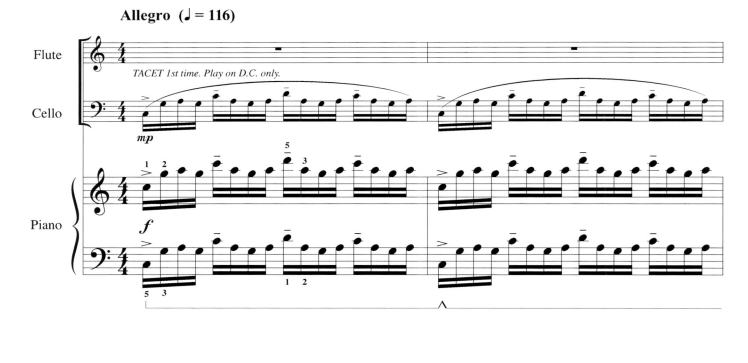

TACET 1st time. Play on D.C. only.

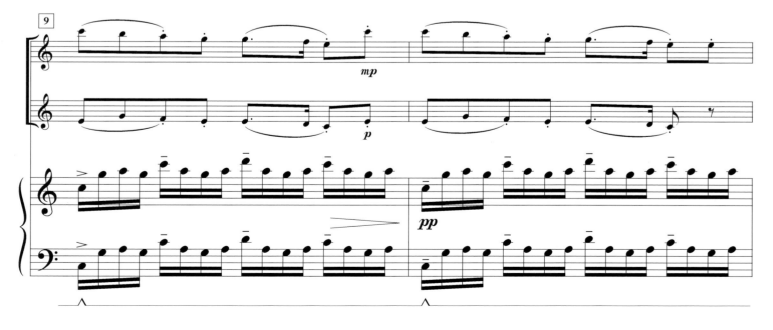

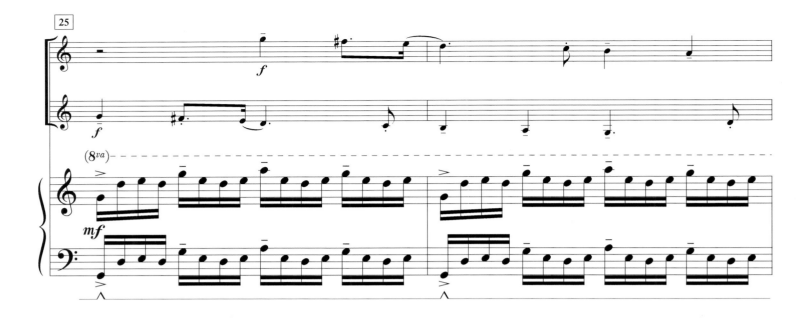

THE COLLABORATIVE ARTIST

Joy to the World

Georg Friedrich Händel

arranged by Nancy Faber

CELLO PART

FABER
PIANO ADVENTURES®

Joy to the World
for Flute, Cello, and Piano

Cello

Georg Friedrich Händel
arranged by Nancy Faber

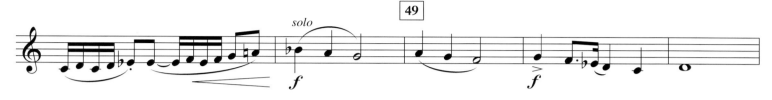

CHAMBER MUSIC SERIES

THE
COLLABORATIVE
Artist

Joy to the World

Georg Friedrich Händel

arranged by **Nancy Faber**

FLUTE PART

FABER
PIANO ADVENTURES

Flute

Joy to the World
for Flute, Cello, and Piano

Georg Friedrich Händel
arranged by Nancy Faber

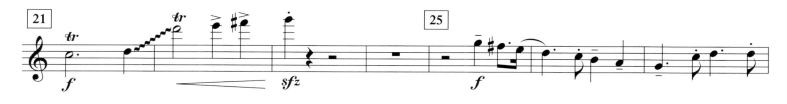

D.C. al Coda

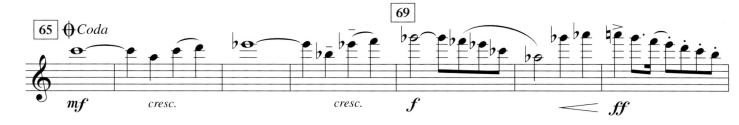

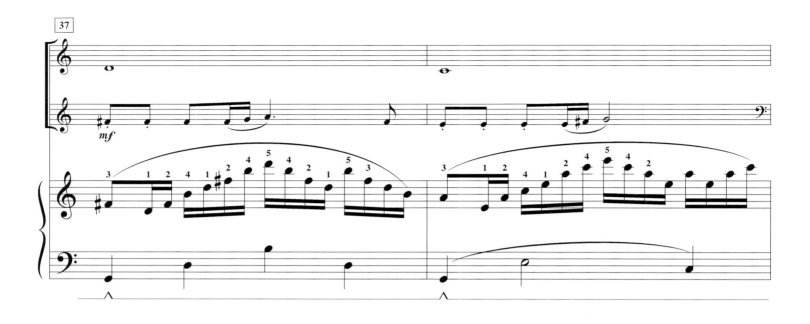

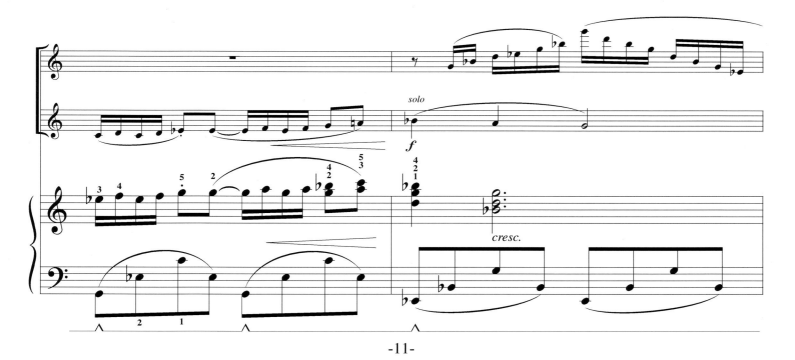

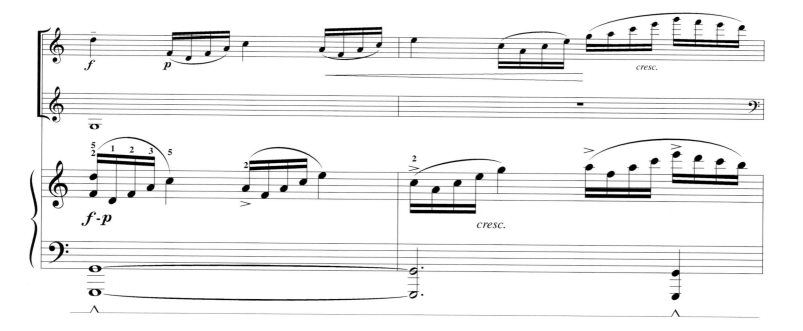

D.C. al Coda

⊕ *Coda*

-14-

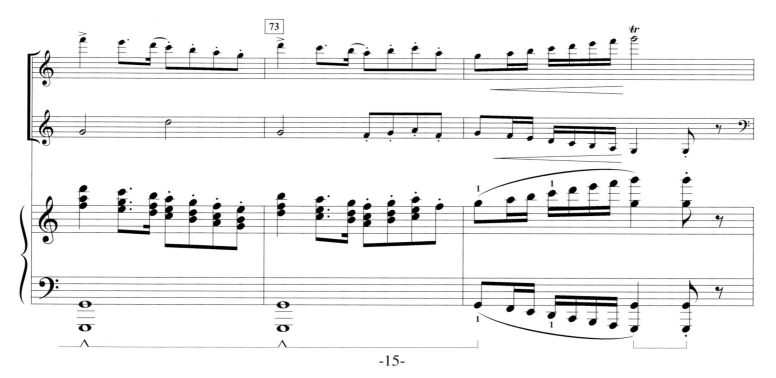

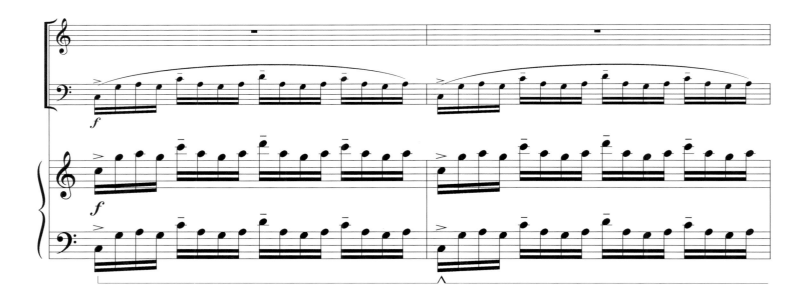

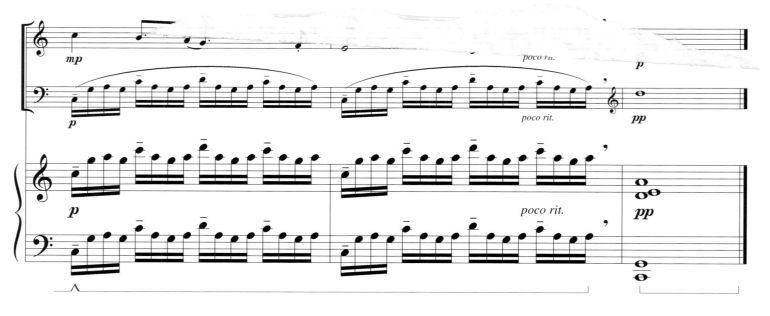